Languages of the World

Bengali

Harriet Milles

www.raintreepublishers.co.uk
Visit our website to find out
more information about
Raintree books.

To order:
☎ Phone 0845 6044371
🖹 Fax +44 (0) 1865 312263
🖻 Email myorders@raintreepublishers.co.uk

Customers from outside the UK please telephone +44 1865 312262

Raintree is an imprint of Capstone Global Library Limited,
a company incorporated in England and Wales having its
registered office at 7 Pilgrim Street, London, EC4V 6LB –
Registered company number: 6695582

Edited by Dan Nunn and Diyan Leake
Designed by Marcus Bell
Original illustrations © Capstone Global Library Ltd 2012
Picture research by Elizabeth Alexander
Originated by Capstone Global Library Ltd
Printed and bound in China by South China Printing
  Company Ltd

ISBN 978 1 406 23283 7 (hardback)
15 14 13 12 11
10 9 8 7 6 5 4 3 2 1

British Library Cataloguing in Publication Data
Milles, Harriet.
  Bengali. -- (Languages of the world)
  491.4'4-dc22
A full catalogue record for this book is available from the
British Library.

Acknowledgements
The author and publisher are grateful to the following for
permission to reproduce copyright material: Alamy pp. 7
(© David Grossman), 12 (© PhotosIndia.com LLC), 13
(© Louise Batalla Duran), 14 (© Danita Delimont), 17
(© Borderlands), 20 (© Borderlands), 22 (© Green Bangla), 23
(© Rphotos), 29 (© Samantha Nundy); Corbis pp. 16 (© Paul
Hackett/In Pictures); Getty Images pp. 9 (Jewel Samad/AFP);
24 (Stu Forster); Getty Images for DAGOC p. 25 (Michael
Steele); Photolibrary pp. 5 (Pawel Libera), 18 (Shehzad
Noorani), 19 (Julio Etchart), 26 (Eye Ubiquitous); Photoshot
p. 28 (Majority World/Mustafiz Mamun); Shutterstock
pp. 6 (© Herr Petroff), 8 (© discpicture), 10 (© jaimaa), 15
(© Darrin Henry), 21 (© fritz16), 27 (© Joe Gough).

Cover photograph of reproduced with permission of Getty
Images (Asia Images Group).

Every effort has been made to contact copyright holders of
material reproduced in this book. Any omissions will be
rectified in subsequent printings if notice is given to the
publisher.

Disclaimer
All the internet addresses (URLs) given in this book were valid
at the time of going to press. However, due to the dynamic
nature of the internet, some addresses may have changed, or
sites may have changed or ceased to exist since publication.
While the author and publisher regret any inconvenience this
may cause readers, no responsibility for any such changes can
be accepted by either the author or the publisher.

Contents

Bengali words in this book are in italics, *like this*.
You can find out how to say them by looking in the
pronunciation guide.

Bengali around the world

Bengali is the main language of the region of Asia known as Bengal. The eastern part of Bengal is now the country of Bangladesh. The western part of Bengal is in India.

India

Bangladesh

Bengali is the main language of the Indian states of West Bengal and Tripura, and the country of Bangladesh.

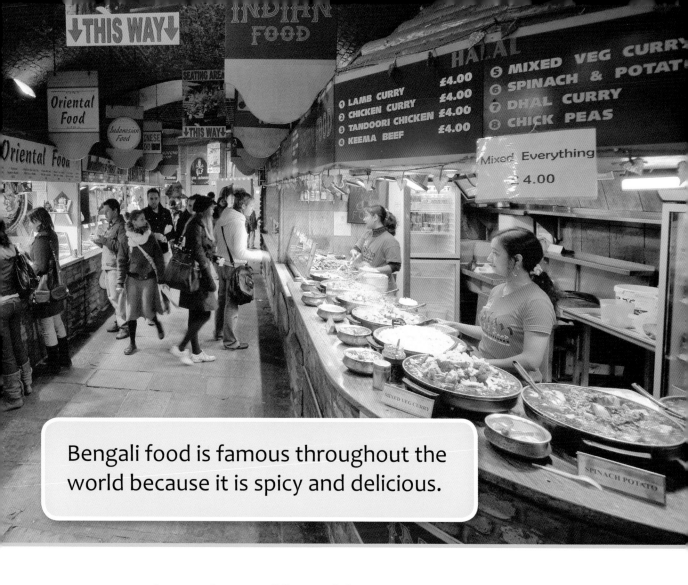

Bengali food is famous throughout the world because it is spicy and delicious.

Bengali is the official language of Bangladesh. There are over 150 million people living in Bangladesh. After Hindi, it is the second most commonly spoken language in India.

Who speaks Bengali?

Over 210 million people around the world speak Bengali as their main language. It is the world's fifth most widely spoken language, after Mandarin Chinese, English, Spanish, and Hindi.

People in this busy market sell flowers for weddings and special feast days.

Family life is very important for Bengalis.

The Bengali language is also called Bangla. Outside Bangladesh and India, there are Bengali speakers living in parts of Nepal, Singapore, Africa, Arabia, the United States, and the United Kingdom.

Bengali and English

Bengali uses a different alphabet to English. English is written on a line with the letters above it. Bengali is written along a line with the letters below it.

Children all around the world learn to read and write.

সারা পৃথিবীতে বাচ্চারা লেখাপড়া শেখে।

shara prithibite bacchara lekhapoṛa shekhe.

This is the same sentence written in English and Bengali.

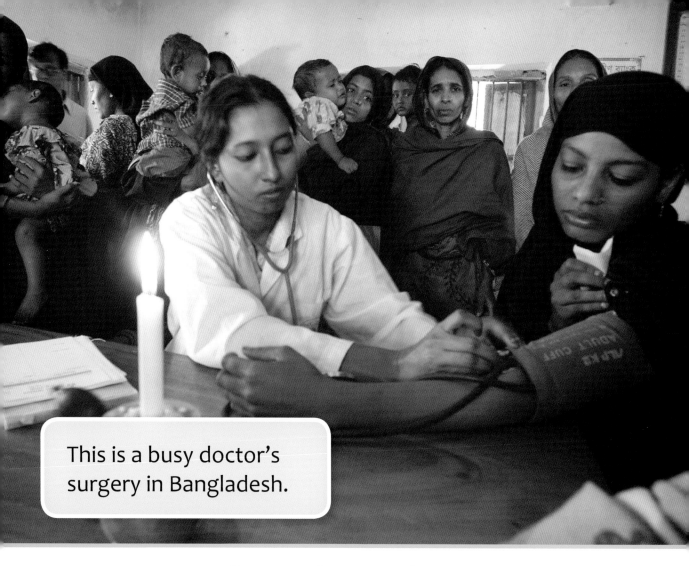

This is a busy doctor's surgery in Bangladesh.

Many Bengali people speak some English. There are words in Bengali that come from English words. For example, "doctor" is *ḍaktar*, "school" is *skul*, and "hospital" is *hashpatal*.

Learning Bengali

The English alphabet has 26 letters. Bengali script has many more letter symbols. So, how can you tell what Bengali script and symbols should sound like?

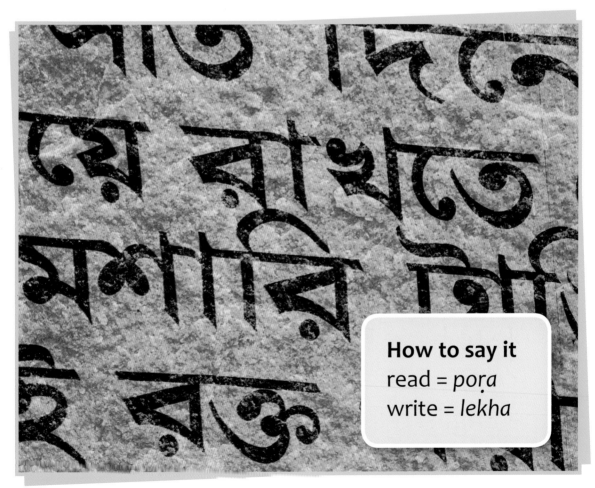

How to say it
read = *poṛa*
write = *lekha*

শুভ জন্মদিন — Bengali script

śubhô jɔnmodin — romanization

shubho jonmodin — pronunciation

Happy Birthday — English

How to say it
English = *Ingreji*

The best way for English-speaking people to learn Bengali is to see how the script would sound if it was written in the English alphabet. This is called "romanization".

Saying hello and goodbye

Bengali people may greet each other by saying, "*Nomoshkar*". They may say, "*Tumi kæmon acho?*", which means "How are you?"

How to say it
hello = *nomoshkar*

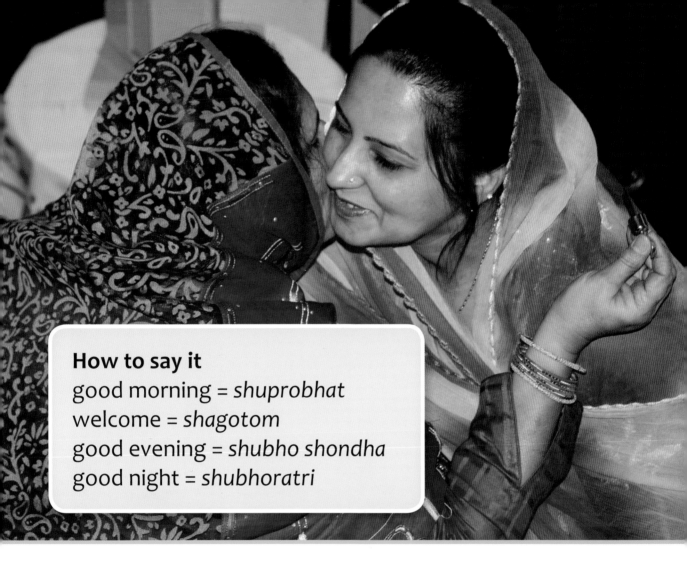

How to say it

good morning = *shuprobhat*

welcome = *shagotom*

good evening = *shubho shondha*

good night = *shubhoratri*

If you are visiting a Bangladeshi or Bengali family, they may say, "*Shagotom!*" which means "Welcome!" When it is time to leave, you might say, "*Abar dækha hobe*", meaning "Goodbye, see you again."

Talking about yourself

When you meet people for the first time, they may ask you for your name. Then you can say, *"Amar nam ..."* ("My name is ... ").

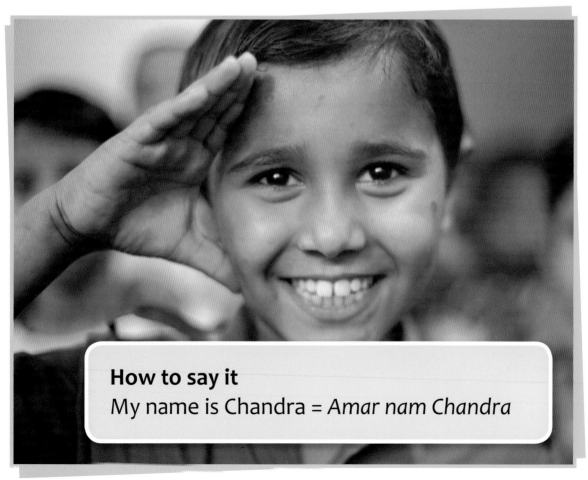

How to say it
My name is Chandra = *Amar nam Chandra*

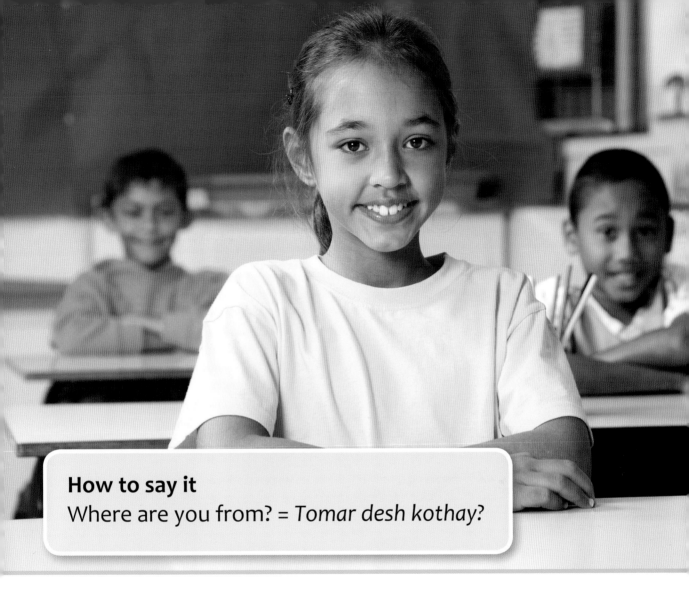

How to say it
Where are you from? = *Tomar desh kothay?*

Then they might ask you where you are from. You might say, "*Ami Laṇḍene thaki*" ("I'm from London"). *Doya kore* means "please" in Bengali.

Asking about others

It is polite to ask people about themselves. The first thing people usually ask is someone's name. You can say, "*Tomar nam ki?*" ("What is your name?")

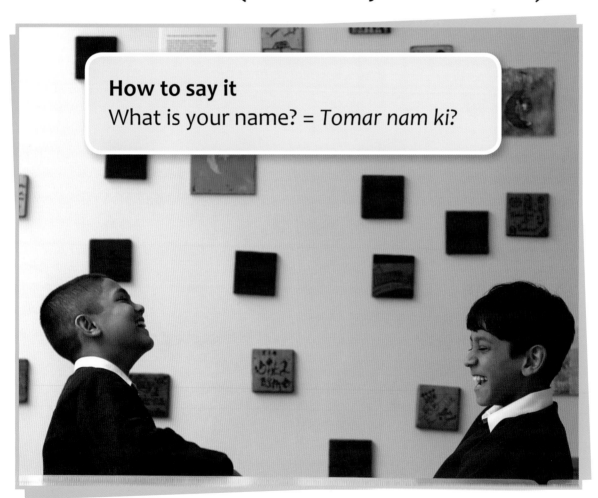

How to say it
What is your name? = *Tomar nam ki?*

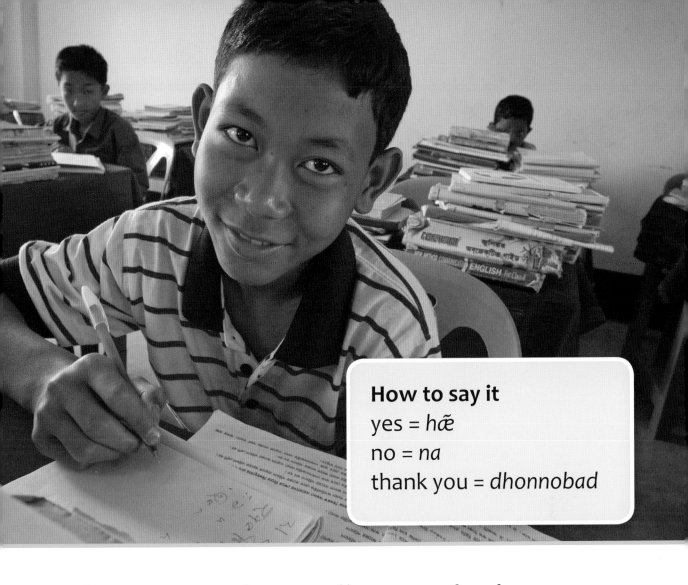

Then you might say, "*Tomar shathe poricito hoye ami khushi hoyechi*" ("I am pleased to meet you"). "Yes" in Bengali is *hǣ*. "No" is *na*. The Bengali for "thank you" is *dhonnobad*.

At home

In country villages in Bangladesh, the houses are built of mud, straw, bamboo, or timber. The most important part of the home is the kitchen area. This is called the *ranna ghor*.

How to say it
village = *gram*
kitchen = *ranna ghor*

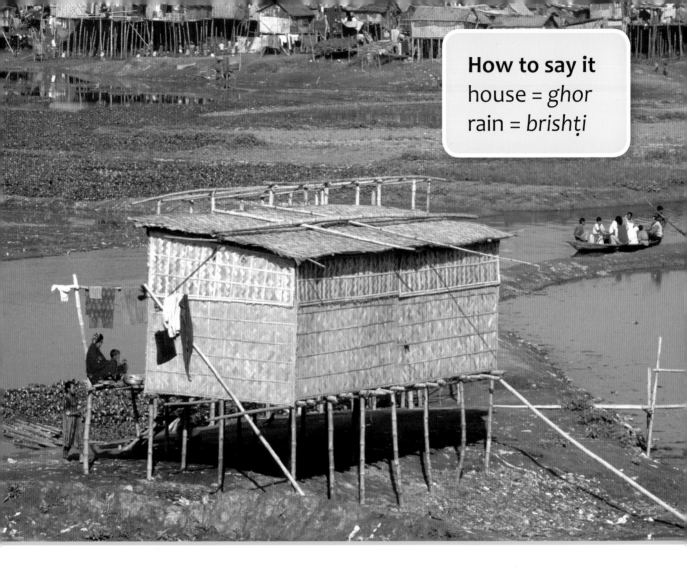

The Bengal region is one of the hottest places in the world. It also has a lot of rain. Some houses near rivers are built on stilts to prevent them from flooding.

Family

Bengali parents, children, aunts, uncles, cousins, and grandparents may all live close together. Their houses may be next to each other and they may share the family kitchen.

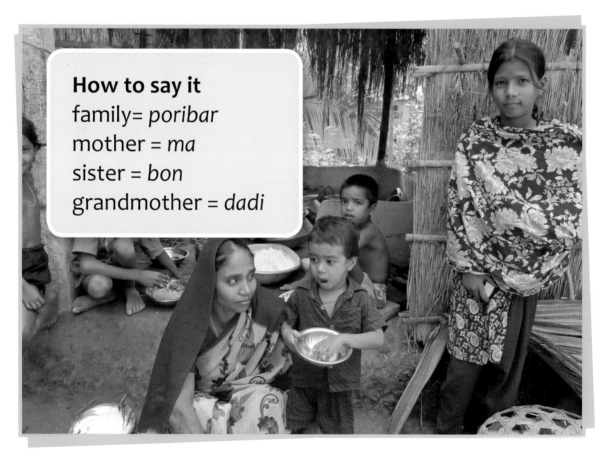

How to say it
family= *poribar*
mother = *ma*
sister = *bon*
grandmother = *dadi*

How to say it
father = *baba*
brother = *bhai*
grandfather = *dada*

Mothers and grandmothers may stay at home to do the cooking, cleaning, and washing. Fathers might do farming or work in towns or cities. A good way to travel to work is in a bicycle taxi called a rickshaw.

At school

In some village schools, children of all ages are taught in one big classroom. They learn to read, write, and do maths. Sometimes they have lessons outdoors, in the shade of trees.

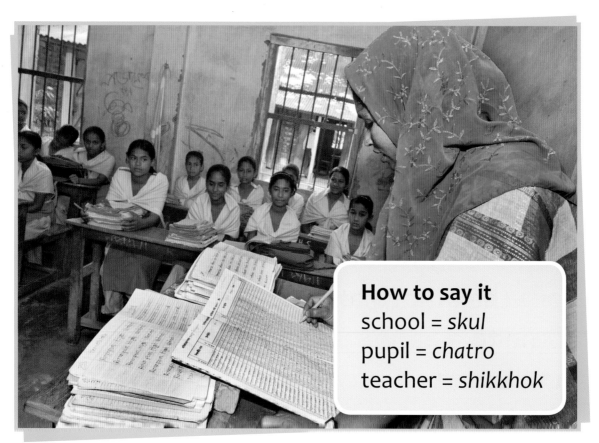

How to say it
school = *skul*
pupil = *chatro*
teacher = *shikkhok*

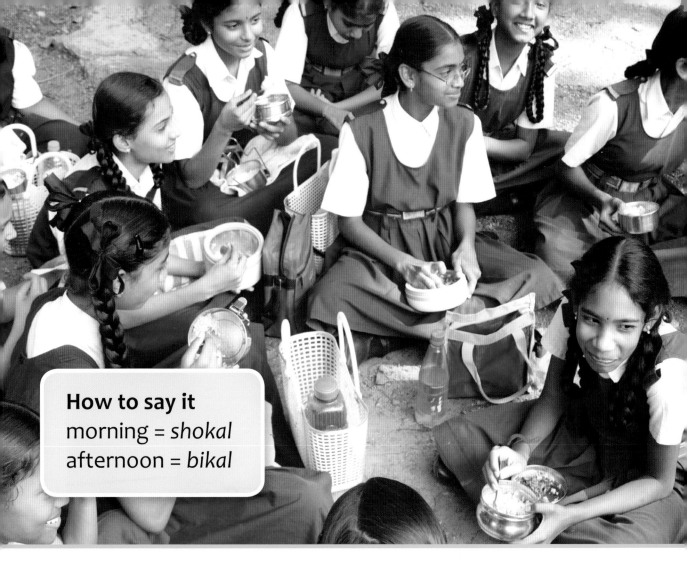

After morning lessons, the children may have their lunch at school. They may go home to eat. Some children from poor families may not go to school because they have to work.

Sport

The most popular games for boys in the Bengal region are cricket and football. Girls may play badminton or netball, but some girls enjoy playing cricket and football, too.

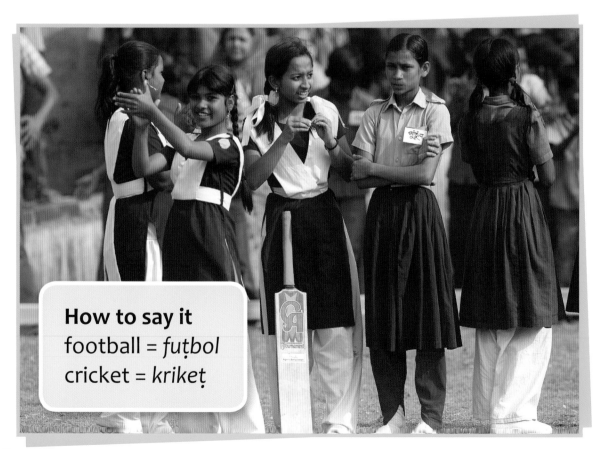

How to say it
football = *fuṭbol*
cricket = *krikeṭ*

How to say it

play = *khæla*

sport = *khæladhula*

team = *dol*

Kabaddi is the national sport of Bangladesh. Two teams have to try to catch one another – and avoid being caught themselves – whilst holding their breath!

Food

Breakfast in Bengal or Bangladesh may be rice, chapatti (a flat piece of bread) with eggs, or some fish. People use their fingers to eat all meals.

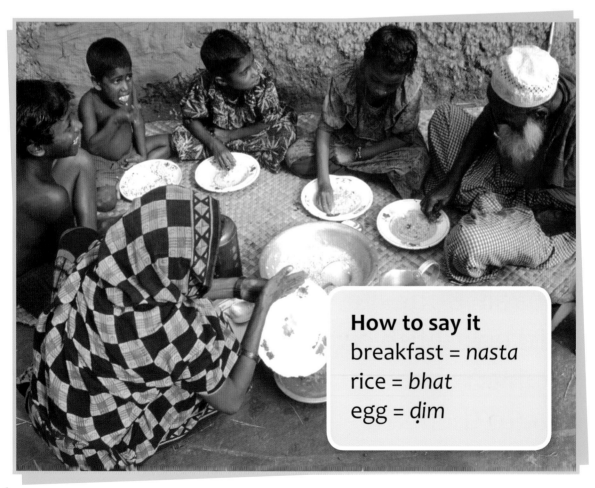

How to say it
breakfast = *nasta*
rice = *bhat*
egg = *ḍim*

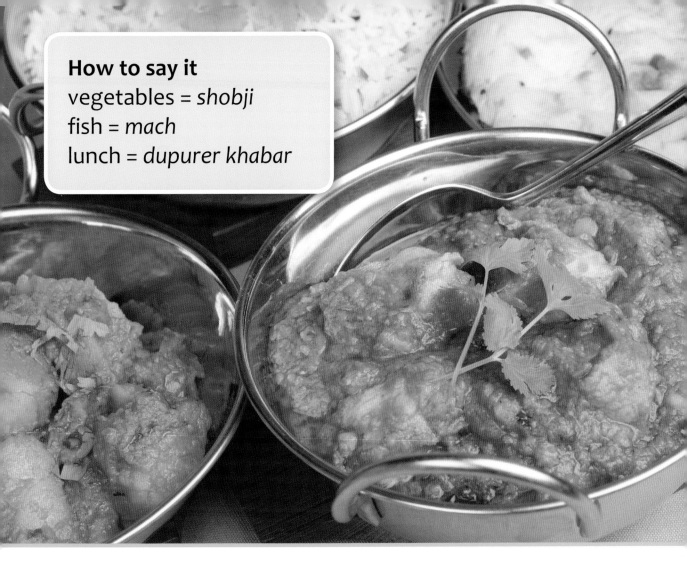

How to say it
vegetables = *shobji*
fish = *mach*
lunch = *dupurer khabar*

Bengali food is very spicy. Vegetable, chicken, or fish curry with rice is a popular lunchtime meal. People also love to drink *cha* (tea) all day long!

Clothes

Children in the Bengal region may wear T-shirts, shorts, or dresses. Girls may wear *shalwar kamiz* (a tunic and trousers). After they are married, they wear a long piece of cloth called a *sari*.

How to say it
dress = *jama*
shoes = *juta*

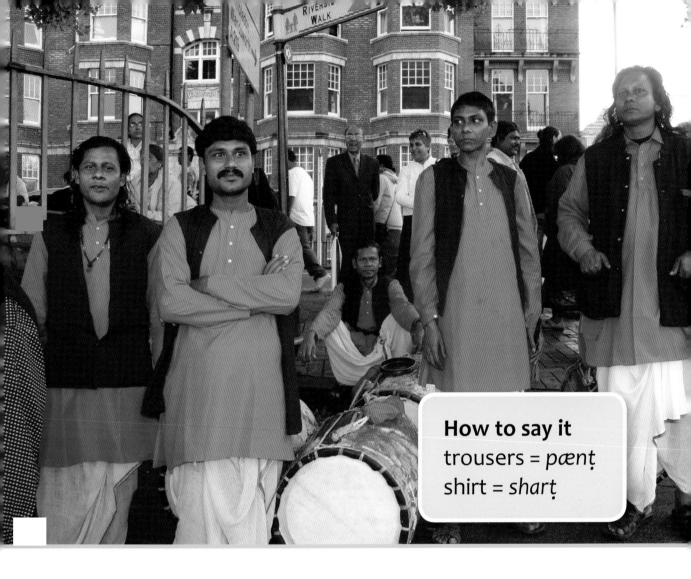

How to say it

trousers = *pænṭ*

shirt = *sharṭ*

In towns, men may wear trousers and shirts. On special occasions, Bengali men may wear a *kurta* (top) and *dhoti*. The *dhoti* is a long piece of white cloth wrapped around the waist.

Pronunciation guide

English	Pronunciation of Bengali word
afternoon	*bikal*
Bengali	*bangla*
breakfast	*nasta*
brother	*bhai*
cricket	*kriket*
doctor	*daktar*
dress	*jama*
egg	*dim*
English	*Ingreji*
family	*poribar*
father	*baba*
fish	*mach*
football	*futbol*
good evening	*shubho shondha*
good morning	*shuprobhat*
good night	*shubhoratri*
goodbye, see you again	*abar dækha hobe*
grandfather	*dada*
grandmother	*dadi*
hello	*nomoshkar*
hospital	*hashpatal*
house	*ghor*
household	*khana*
How are you?	*Tumi kæmon acho?*
I am pleased to meet you.	*Tomar shathe poricito hoye ami khushi hoyechi.*
I'm from London.	*Ami Landene thaki.*

kitchen	*ranna ghor*
lunch	*dupurer khabar*
morning	*shokal*
mother	*ma*
My name is ...	*Amar nam ...*
no	*na*
play	*khæla*
please	*doya kore*
pupil	*chatro*
rain	*brishṭi*
read	*poṛa*
rice	*bhat*
school	*skul*
shirt	*shart*
shoes	*juta*
sister	*bon*
sport	*khæladhula*
tea	*cha*
teacher	*shikkhok*
team	*dol*
thank you	*dhonnobad*
trousers	*pænṭ*
vegetables	*shobji*
village	*gram*
welcome	*shagotom*
What is your name?	*Tomar nam ki?*
Where are you from?	*Tomar desh kothay?*
write	*lekha*
yes	*hæ̃*

1 = æk, 2 = dui, 3 = tin, 4 = car, 5 = pãc, 6 = choy, 7 = shat, 8 = at, 9 = noy, 10 = dosh

31

Find out more

Books

India (Destination Detectives), Anita Roy (Raintree, 2006)

India (Discover Countries), Tim Atkinson (Wayland, 2010)

Living in Bangladesh, Ruth Thomson (Sea to Sea
    Publications, 2007)

Star Children's Picture Dictionary: English-Bengali, Babita Verma
    (Star Publications/Languages of the World Publication, 2006)

Website

www.timeforkids.com/TFK/kids/news/story/0,28277,1932891,00.
html

Find out how floating schools are changing kids' lives in
Bangladesh.

Index

alphabet 8, 10, 11
Bangladesh 4, 7, 18, 25, 26
Bengal region 4, 19, 24, 26, 28
family 7, 13, 20
India 4, 7
languages 4, 5, 6, 7